MRS. DOWDY SAID...

"Home-spun Theology of Folk Wisdom"

By
Angelee Coleman Grider

MRS. DOWDY SAID...

"Home-spun Theology of Folk Wisdom"

by

Angelee Coleman Grider

Subtitle given by Rev. Cleveland Ohio Wilkins (Holly Springs, MS)
Insert contributions by JoAnn Watson (Olive Branch, MS)
Referenced Scriptures – Holy Bible – The African American Jubilee Edition (King James Version)

Photo usage – PublicDomainImages.com
Photo usage – Creative Commons and PublicDomainPictures.net

ISBN-13: 978-0983032519   978-0-9820354-5-0

Preface

What did your mom or grandmother say that seemed to be a "little illogical"?

Ancestors would declare that "The Bible said…" even when the statement was not straight from the scriptures.

Yet the wisdom was meant to wean us off bad habits, or steer us onward to better lives than that of which the ancestors lived.

By studying some of the renditions though, it appeared to me that, with all good intentions, the elderly had profoundly studied the words of the Bible, listened to the preacher on Sunday mornings, and combined mental brawns, wit and of course understanding, with their own ways or application of ruling their household.

The book is not meant to be judgmental. These are some "shared" thoughts. The followings are only few of so many statements and procedures for how they related to the true word of God, Jesus or The Holy Spirit.

Photo by Angelee Coleman Grider

The mind is like an uncultivated lot —ready for renovation.

(A. Coleman Grider)

Introduction

Mrs. Dowdy was a woman of natural cures, a woman with a wistful-tongue language, and was one who had insightful intuitions. I remember the real Mrs. Dowdy. When she spoke in her quiet toned voice, everyone listened. Her wisdom was not to be surpassed by any means, yet America itself has a rich heritage of customs. That's what Mrs. Dowdy said.

Ancestors would declare oh so often that "The Bible said…" even when the statement was not straight from the scriptures. Yet the wisdom was meant to be used to wean us off bad habits, or steer us onward to much better lives than the lifestyle of which they lived.

Remembering and studying some of the renditions though, it appeared to me that, with all good intentions, the elderly had profoundly studied the words of the Bible, listened to the preacher on Sunday mornings, and combined mental brawns, wit, and understanding with their own application of ruling their household. The followings are only few of so many statements and procedures for how they related to the true word of God, Jesus or The Holy Spirit.

List Price: **$7.95**

5" x 8" (12.7 x 20.32 cm)

M.O.R.E. Publishers, Memphis (TN)

ISBN-13: **978-0983032519**

ISBN-10: **0983032513**

BISAC: Body, Mind & Spirit / General

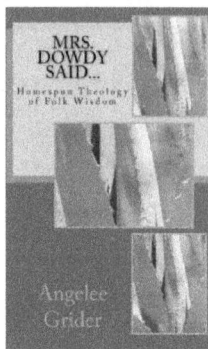

This book is dedicated to all those who were "street wise"

like Mrs. Dowdy.

"Your cup runneth over with love. "

MRS. DOWDY SAID…

"Home-spun Theology of Folk Wisdom"

Compiled by

Angelee Coleman Grider

- A grave must be 6 feet long and 6 feet wide.

(God will help us if the person is longer than that.)

- A hard head makes a soft booty.

- All that glitters ain't gold.

("Beware of false prophets.")
(Exodus 23-6-8 - Keep thee far from a false matter; and the innocent and righteous slay thou not: for I will not justify the wicked.)

- An apple a day keeps the doctor away.

(Acts 27:34 - Wherefore I pray you to take some meat: for this is for your health: for there shall not an hair fall from the head of any of you.)

- An empty wagon makes a lot of noise.

(Proverbs 30:8 - Remove far from me vanity and lies: give me neither poverty nor riches; feed me with food convenient for me.)

(Exodus 32:18 - And he said, It is not the voice of them that shout for mastery, neither is it the voice of them that cry for being overcome: but the noise of them that sing do I hear.)

- A frown is nothing but an up-side down smile.

(Isaiah 61:9-11 - I will greatly rejoice in the LORD, my soul shall be joyful in my God; for he hath clothed me with the garments of salvation, he hath covered me with the robe of righteousness, as a bridegroom decketh himself with ornaments, and as a bride adorneth herself with her jewels.)

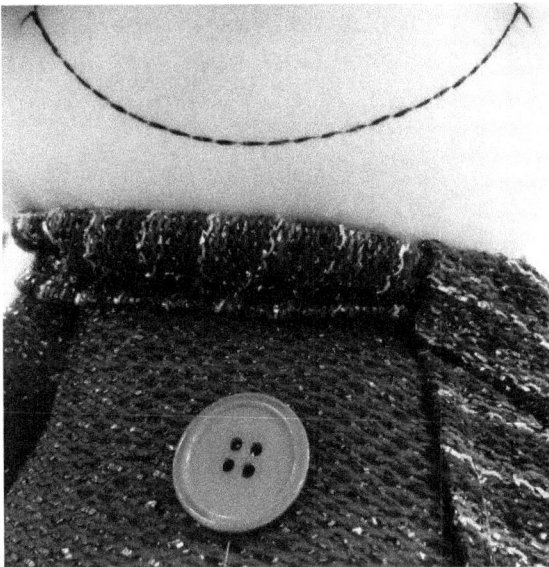

- An apple does not fall far from the tree.

(Genesis 1:11 - And God said, Let the earth bring forth grass, the herb yielding seed, and the fruit tree yielding fruit after his kind, whose seed is in itself, upon the earth: and it was so.)

(Genesis 1:12 - And the earth brought forth grass, and herb yielding seed after his kind, and the tree yielding fruit, whose seed was in itself, after his kind: and God saw that it was good.)

- An ounce of prevention is worth a pound of cure.

●

(Genesis 3:3 - But of the fruit of the tree which is in the midst of the garden, God hath said, Ye shall not eat of it, neither shall ye touch it, lest ye die.)

(Genesis 3:13 - And the LORD God said unto the woman, What is this that thou hast done? And the woman said, The serpent beguiled me, and I did eat. And unto Adam he said, Because thou hast hearkened unto the voice of thy wife, and hast eaten of the tree, of which I commanded thee, saying, Thou shalt not eat of it: cursed is the ground for thy sake; in sorrow shalt thou eat of it all the days of thy life;…)

- A stitch in time saves nine.

(Genesis 29:34 - And she conceived again, and bare a son; and said, Now this time will my husband be joined unto me, because I have born him three sons: therefore was his name called Levi.)

(Leviticus 13:58 - And the garment, either warp, or wool, or whatsoever thing of skin it be, which thou shalt wash, if the plague be departed from them, then it shall be washed the second time, and shall be clean.)

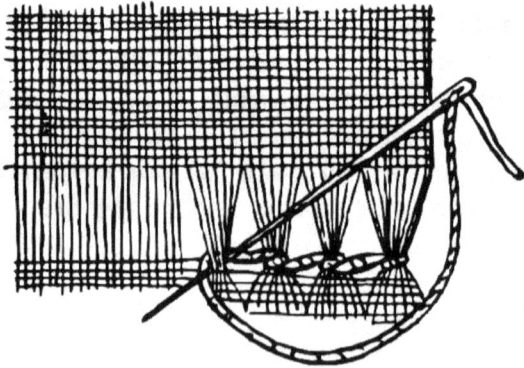

- Be a true friend to the child next door. We all need someone to talk to sometimes.

(Proverbs 17:17 – A friend loveth at all times…)

- Be aware of wolves in sheep clothing.

(Matthew 7:15 - Beware of false prophets, which come to you in sheep's clothing, but inwardly they are ravening wolves.)

(2 Samuel 14:2 - And Joab sent to Tekoah, and fetched thence a wise woman, and said unto her, I pray thee, feign thyself to be a mourner, and put on now mourning apparel, and anoint not thyself with oil, but be as a woman that had a long time mourned for the dead:...)

- Big Brother is watching you.

- Before I let you... you will burn in hell.

- Born after daybreak, you die before nightfall.

(*Job 4:20 - Born after daybreak, you die before nightfall and disappear forever.*) *Contemporary English Version*

- Parent spoke these words to a boy/girl - I'll slap you into next year.

(Proverbs 22:6 - Train up a child in the way he should go: and when he is old, he will not depart from it.)

- Call a spade a spade.

(Matthew 5:37 - But let your communication be, Yea, yea; Nay, nay: for whatsoever is more than these cometh of evil.)

- Change your underwear every day. You never know when an emergency may come. Even though they will cut your under-wear off, at least the underwear will be clean.

- Cleanliness is next to Godliness.

- Dip your biscuit while your gravy is hot.

(Genesis 18:5 - And I will fetch a morsel of bread, and comfort ye your hearts; after that ye shall pass on: for therefore are ye come to your servant. And they said, "So do, as thou hast said.")

- Do not let this harvest pass.

(Genesis 19:17 - And it came to pass, when they had brought them forth abroad, that he said, Escape for thy life; look not behind thee, neither stay thou in all the plain; escape to the mountain, lest thou be consumed.)

- Don't let your right hand know what your left hand is doing.

(Genesis 4:5 - But unto Cain and to his offering he had not respect. And Cain was very wroth, and his countenance fell.)

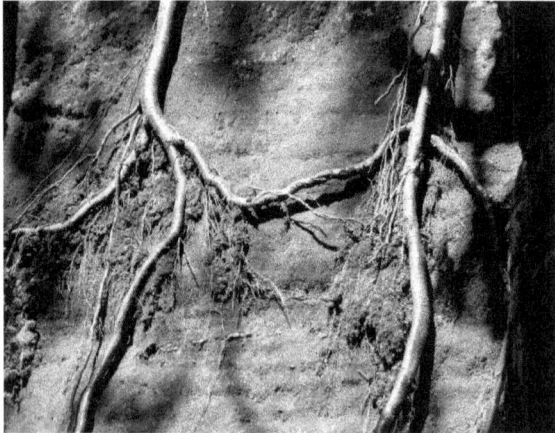

- Don't change horses in the middle of a stream.

(Genesis 20:5 - Said he not unto me, She is my sister? and she, even she herself said, He is my brother: in the integrity of my heart and innocency of my hands have I done this.

(Genesis 20:6 - And God said unto him in a dream, Yea, I know that thou didst this in the integrity of thy heart; for I also withheld thee from sinning against me: therefore suffered I thee not to touch her.)

- Don't put off for tomorrow what you can do today.

(Genesis 7:4 - For yet seven days, and I will cause it to rain upon the earth forty days and forty nights; and every living substance that I have made will I destroy from off the face of the earth.)

- Every dog has got his day.

(Job 24:22-25 - Even if they seem successful, they are doomed to fail.)

- Every tub got to sit on its own bottom.

(Job 21:26 - But we all end up dead, beneath a blanket of worms.)

(Isaiah 45:23 - I have sworn by myself, the word is gone out of my mouth in righteousness, and shall not return, That unto me every knee shall bow, every tongue shall swear.)

- Feed an enemy with a long-handled spoon.

(*Genesis 31:1-3 - And Jacob beheld the countenance of Laban, and, behold, it was not toward him as before.*)

(*Genesis 31:5 - And said unto them, I see your father's countenance, that it is not toward me as before; but the God of my father hath been with me.*)

(*Genesis 31:7 - And your father hath deceived me, and changed my wages ten times; but God suffered him not to hurt me.*)

(*Genesis 31:15 - Are we not counted of him strangers? For he hath sold us, and hath quite devoured also our money.*)

- Go through the tunnel.

(Psalms 91:4-5 - He shall cover thee with his feathers, and under his wings shalt thou trust; his truth shall be thy shield and buckler.)

(Psalms 91:5 Thou shalt not be afraid for the terror by night; nor for the arrow that flieth by day...)

- God rains on the just as well as the unjust.

(*Job 9:22 - What difference does it make? God destroys the innocent along with the guilty.*)

- **God built you that way.**

(Proverbs 23: 24 – The father of the righteous shall greatly rejoice: and he that begetteth a wise child shall have joy of him.)

- He's got the whole world in His hands.

(*Job 12: 10 - Every living creature is in the hands of God.*)

- Honesty is the best policy.

- I have a bone to pick with you.

- If it walks like a duck, it's a duck.

- If a duck keeps his bib shut, he'll never get caught.

- If you dig one ditch, you better dig two.

- I'm not your brother's keeper.

(Genesis 4:9 - Am I my brother's keeper...?)

- In unity, there is strength.

- It is better to have and not need, than to need and not have.

- Keep a HIGH self-esteem. (Love yourself).

- Know yourself.

- Let lying dogs lay.

- Let your conscience be your guide.

- Life is a precious thing.

- Life is short, but sweet.

- Money is the root of all evil.

The love of money is the root of all evil.

- My grave should be turned facing the East so I'll be ready when my Jesus comes.

- No ifs, ands, or buts about it.

(Matthew 5:37 - But let your communication be, Yea, yea; Nay, nay: for whatsoever is more than these cometh of evil.)

- Nobody can make you stop — only you!

- One life to live? I'm gonna' live it.
- Our sins are buried in the sea of God's forgetfulness.

- Parents are not perfect.

- Remember: Memories fade, but love lasts forever.
  (December 30, 2014 - A. Coleman Grider)

- …Rob Peter to pay Paul.

- Some people are like a refrigerator. "They can't keep anything for long."

- Strut your stuff.

- That's just the blind leading the blind.

- There is a season for all things.

- Jesus stated that when you see these things happening…

- There are two (2) sides to every story. In between the two you will find the truth.

- The early bird catches the worm.

- There is more than one way to skin a cat.

- Think twice before you speak.

Matthew 5:37 - But let your communication be, Yea, yea; Nay, nay: for whatsoever is more than these cometh of evil.

- Treat people the way that you want to be treated.

(Matthew 7:11-12 - If ye then, being evil, know how to give good gifts unto your children, how much more shall your Father which is in heaven give good things to them that ask him?)

(Therefore all things whatsoever ye would that men should do to you, do ye even so to them: for this is the law and the prophets.)

- …Turn the other cheek.

(Matthew 5:39 - but I say unto you, That ye resist not evil; but whosoever shall smite thee on thy right cheek, turn to him the other also.)

- ***Turn around. Don't Drown!***

(Austen Onek, 2015 TV weather, WREG) If you see a puddle of water, don't be foolish enough to ruin your car by trying to go through it. Turn around and go another way. You might be late for your appointment, but you won't be going there dead.

- Two wrongs don't make no right.

- Do unto others as you would have them do unto you.

- Use what you got.

(Take what you have, and use what you got. Don't keep looking for something else.)

- What's done in the dark will come to the light.

(Matthew 4:16 - the people which sat in darkness saw great light; and to them which sat in the region and shadow of death, light is sprung up.)

- When a child saw a lady pregnant she asked, "What is wrong?" Someone replied, "She broke her leg". Another answered, "She stumped her toe."

- We all been young. We all had problems. It won't come out overnight.

- When thunder roars, go indoors. (Austen Onek, 2014)

If you can hear thunder, it's too close for you to be outside. The lightening will flash soon, and lightning has no boundaries of where it will strike. Don't take a chance and be a target. Don't stand under a tree either. Trees are big attractions for lightening.

- You are as slow as molasses.

Maple Syrup Trees (SAP)

- You better catch the first wagon going out of here.

If yours is not working, you can't be choicy. Get a ride and get going.

- You don't bite the hand that feeds you.

Be particular about how you treat people.

- You don't look a gift horse in the mouth.

- You don't miss your water 'til your well runs dry.

- You must care about yourself.

- You need to clean up your own house before you can clean up mine.

(Matthew 7:3-4 - And why beholdest thou the mote that is in thy brother's eye, but considerest not the beam that is in thine own eye?)

Mrs. Dowdy's Prayer

Now I lay me down to sleep.

I pray to the Lord my soul to keep.

If I should die before I wake,

I pray to the Lord my soul to take.

This I ask in Jesus' name

Amen

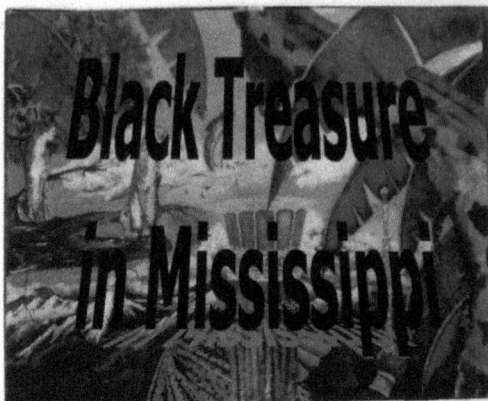

Black Treasure
In Mississippi

And The Best of Revival Songs

Revised Edition

Florence Virginia Wilkins Coleman

Food for Thought - Your plan:

God has a plan for everyone, and He has a plan for you.
He'll guide your life 'til day is done. And will always see you through.

God has a goal for you to reach, and a life that He wants you to live.

He has a child

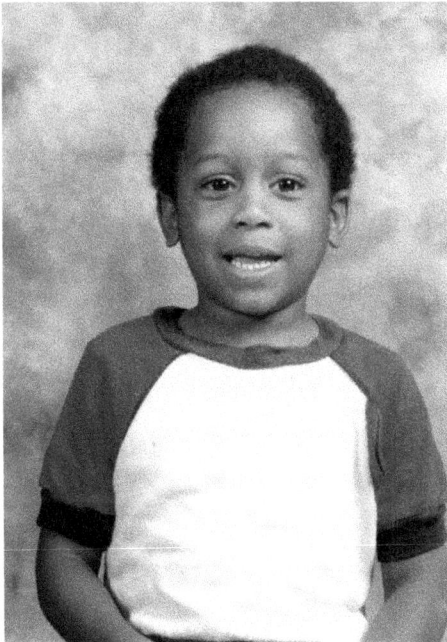

Edwin Marcellus T. Grider, St. Louis (MO), 3

for you to teach, and there's help that you need to give.

God has a star to light your way, as He guides in the path of His will.

He will give you strength for every day.

As your heart, with His Love He fills.

Food for Thought - An Ode To M.I. (Mississippi Industrial College, 1940's)

MISSISSIPPI INDUSTRIAL COLLEGE, HOLLY SPRINGS, MISS.

44 Original Poems

(excerpts)
Compiled by Classmate

F.V.W. Coleman

My Pet

By
Carrie L. Barnes

I

I have a pet under the tree,
Who likes to lie real close to me,
And turn his merry little nose,
And wriggles his five little toes.

II
He always plays out in the sun,
And never knows what must be done.
He's just as jolly as can be.
I love this pet as you may see.

Keep Going
by
Bonnie Gordan

I

There is always just one more round.
So friend, don't stop to fret and frown.
Just start your step and walk on top,
Until it's best for you to stop.

II

Sometimes the cool wind may not blow.
Don't let your cares make you go slow.
There is a prize to all the wise,
So friend press on what'er be tide.

Bedtime

I
Come children, put away your toys.
The day is done for girls and boys.
Come now dear ones and let us pray,
For now it is the end of day.

II
So get your night gown. Please don't
fret, or else your milk you will not get.
And on tomorrow, you may go
To see you friend that loves you so.

My Pet
by
Ollie Covington

I
I have a cat. His name is mask.
He is always busy all day,
Because he has a daily task.
He likes to keep the rats away.

II
All of the children love our cat.
Each day with him, they like to play.
They want to help him find a rat,
And when it's night they all go away.

Then and Now
By
Irma Green

I

As I went out the door today,
I saw some children run and play.
It made me think about the time,
When I would play 'til bell would chime.

II

But now that age of life is thru,
I have some other things to do.
Why life is dull, but sometime gay…?
There is more work than there is play.

Tulips
by
Virgie Lester

I

I love to see the Tulips in May,
to watch the birds in spring all day.
That's when the trees begin to grow.
The tulips come out in a row.

II

And when the rain begins to fall,
the tulips then will grow real TALL.
When all birds begin to sing,
Then you will know it is spring.

A Fish
By
Mrs. Bell

I

I caught a fish. His name is Flip.
He likes to flap and flop, and skip.
But Flip will swim with me each day,
Because he likes to dive and play.

II

My Flip is very smart and bold.
He always helps me reach my goal.
At last when work has been all done,
We start again to have some fun.

Sleeping Susan
By
Celestine Hughes

I

There was a girl who always slept,
Awfully late each morning and night.
This little girl, she had no pep,
And she was not so very bright.

II

One day her mother said to her,
"Susan dear, now listen to me.
If you just only pray daughter,
Your illness would leave you all free."

Dancing
By
Margaret Barksdale

I

When I was ten I kept in time,
From one to eight, then eight to nine;
With modern steps such as the Twist,
Because it was hard to resist.

II

Mother called me to eat my lunch,
But all I did was drink my punch.
I went out with a pony step, and
Mom came for me with the big belt.

The Little Boat
by
Mildred Adrain

I

This morning as I went to school,
I passed a little swimming pool
to see a boat without an oar,
go sailing to the other shore.

II

What fun I thought to have a ride,
and look upon the other side.
But I could not do it at all.
The little boat was much too small.

Oration: "What Makes A Home? by Florence W. Coleman

They say there is no place like home, and I believe it's true. No other spot in all the world looks half as good to you.

Although it may be humble, and although it may be small, there's something there that satisfies, and it is home. That's all

Now really it is not the house or barn or yard. I guess that makes you so contented and bring such happiness.

So I have wondered what it is that makes a home so fair. I've about made up my mind. It's just because

Mother is there. (Give a token of flowers). 'Tis mother's Day so unto you, a token of flowers we give with a wish that your pathway may ever be bright as long as you live.

They (the flowers) tell of our love for you always. They tell of the Father's care. They tell that He will watch over you each day, and crown you with blessings fair.

A home would never be a home without a mother dear to fill the place with tender love and hope and trusting cheer.

A Mother brightens every day with sunshine — warm and fair. It

may be raining with rain outside, but it
is pleasant there.

Her smile is like a sun-lit ray
that shines from heaven above. Her
eyes are like glowing stars revealing a
heart of tender love.

A home would never be the
same without a Mother there. So I
will try to make each day of Mother's
life more fair.

The Menu
(Wednesday)

Pan-fried chicken

Mashed sweet potatoes

Mixed greens

Carrot strips

Cornmeal muffins

Milk

Visit our websites:
www.morepublishers.biz

http://StirUpTheGiftEnterprise.com/
www.TheScaleMagazine.MagCloud.com

www.CafePress.com/MOREPublishers

www.ArtistRising.com/galleries/HoltUpChurchandWilkins

www.MemphisHolt.artistrising.com/

www.CDBaby.com www.Spotify.com

Favorite Affiliates
www.FWColemanTheatre.com

Veterans Forever – A Proud Hero (youtube.com)

Family Writers:

Della Bernice Wilkins Wadsworth Phillips

Rev. Cleveland Ohio Wilkins

Fannie Belle Wilkins Lebby

Florence V.W. Coleman, Nina M. Wilkins Hitchings,
Angelee C. Grider, Christopher Earl Grider

This Is My "Will"

How to Write Obiographical Sketches
[Your Own Obituaries]

Angelee Coleman Grider and Lizzie B. Davis

AMAZING

Animals
OF THIS
LAND

A Book of Poetry for Children

Angelee Coleman Grider

Selected Readings
Angelee Coleman-Grider